Your Money.
Your Business.

6 Business Principles to Advance Your Personal Finances

by
Jeremiah Jones

Diminished 7th LC

To my mom,
who taught me fiscal responsibility…

…whether I wanted it or not.

Contents

Introduction

Conversations about personal finance can be uncomfortable and often conclude with an attitude of "it's none of your business!" Even worse, we not only tend to avoid the topic with others, but sometimes find ourselves ignoring (or inadequately addressing) the way our financial matters affect our lives. This needs to change! Easier said than done...

This is *your* life, *your* finances and is very much *your business*. Your finances are *your* business not only in the sense that you have control and ownership over financial decisions, but also because you can indeed manage your finances like a CEO (Chief Executive Officer) manages a company.

This book seeks to drive that point home by teaching principles of great personal finance through fundamental business concepts. If a business can apply principles of financial wisdom to create a strong foundation for wealth and growth, can an individual do the same? The answer is an absolute "yes!"

This book will cover the basic concepts of business finance in a way that is easy to understand and apply. Using analogies, examples, and fun illustrations (thanks to my 10-year old daughter!) we will explore a few basic financial principles that have guided successful companies for centuries, perhaps for millennia!

I should be clear about what this book is NOT intended to be... this book is not a get-rich-quick instruction manual, nor is the focus on becoming wealthy. It is not a guidebook to personal wealth, a recipe for growing a business, or tips & tricks for saving pennies.

This book is about seeing your financial life through a new set of lenses – a fresh perspective. It is about learning basic financial principles that support successful businesses, and how you can apply those same principles to your personal finances. As the old adage goes, "money doesn't buy happiness", but unwise handling of money can lead to misery while wise handling of money brings peace of mind.

As your financial wisdom advances, you will find greater satisfaction from handling your finances; you will feel more confident and in control of your financial decisions; and ultimately, you will be better equipped to put your money to use where it belongs: in reaching your life's ultimate goals.

Chapter 1

The 6 Principles

T here are thousands of books about business published today and just about as many ideas on how to help businesses make money. With all these differing opinions and ideas about what is critical to good business, there is one thing that everyone can agree on: managing money is critical to making money. All successful companies have at least that one thing in common; they are not only good at making money, but at *managing* it as well.

While this is not a book about how to run a business, we are going to investigate six of the fundamental money management philosophies that guide great businesses and discover how we can apply those same principles to personal finance. Commercial enterprises have been refining principles of economics and finance for millennia. Why not take advantage of that progress and put that knowledge to use in the way we approach personal and family finances? Applying key business principles to our own money will afford us the same advantage wise money management offers corporations – the foundation to build a stable financial future while balancing the needs and desires of the present.

Specifically, we will look at six key principles that guide modern business finance and will see how those same principles can just as easily guide personal and family financial matters.

The six principles are:

1 Know Your Destination
2 Mind Your Shareholders
3 Time Changes Value
4 Money Seeds Money
5 See Tomorrow, Today
6 Spending Closes Doors

Occasionally we will talk about our finances as being a journey, one that was probably started a while ago. On this journey, we have a destination, roads to travel, traveling companions, a vehicle, fuel, and various obstacles along the way. We will also be frequently referring to a fictitious business, HappyLiving Incorporated, which will be described more in the next chapter.

The principles outlined in this book are well established concepts in the world of business and are used to help companies grow in their own financial journey of corporate development. We are going to borrow these timeless principles to run our own finances like a business and speed us along our financial journey.

Chapter 2

Principle 1:
Know Your Destination

Key Concepts

❖ Having a vision/mission, a sense of your life's higher purpose
❖ Money is an engine for growth, not a destination

O ur first two principles will establish the "why" and "who" of financial decision-making. Without a solid foundation upon which to build better decision-making, we may struggle to keep a solid financial structure in place. With that in mind, let's continue our financial journey in the same place that successful companies do today, with a *mission* (the "why").

Money is not (or at least, should not be) the end-all be-all of either a company or individual. Great companies exists for a higher purpose and have non-monetary goals guiding the vision of the organization. Take, for example, FranklinCovey, a training and consulting company whose mission statement is "we enable greatness in people and organizations everywhere..." And they really mean it! They retain that mission statement in their minds as they make critical decisions for the company. Likewise, our lives should be guided by a sense of higher purpose that brings us non-monetary satisfaction with life. This "higher purpose" is the destination of our journey. The first principle is to "Know Your Destination."

If money is not the ultimate goal of a business, why is it so important to the success of a company and why is money one of the primary ways of measuring the success of a business? The answer to this question is that growth and success require resources. A great mission, alone, has little effect on the world; but with the right resources, a business can move forward and progress. For a business, those resources include **people** who need to be paid to provide for themselves and their families; they include **materials** to make products or to perform a service; and they include **intangibles** (things that we can't touch) like knowledge, data, or services from other companies.

All of these things require money. Money provides the vehicle through which a business can grow, thrive, and accomplish its mission. As a result, it makes perfect sense that over thousands of years of seeing entire economies come and go, businesses have refined and improved their ability to make money. Indeed, at the heart of every great company is a refined, optimized, and intelligent method for handling the finances of the business.

When it comes to personal and family finances, our situation is the same. We ought to have a "higher purpose" to our lives. Imagine a road trip... just as the engine of a car may be necessary to reach our destination, money can act as a resource to fuel our life's journey; and just as the engine of the car is not the ultimate goal of a road trip, money should not be the destination for our lives.

We can manage our finances in a way that maximizes our ability to achieve the things in life that matter the most to us.

To do that, let's start with a job promotion – *your* promotion! You are now the CEO (Chief Executive Officer) of your life. Congratulations! From here on out, the principles in this book can be used to guide your financial choices and assist in setting you up to accomplish the great things in your future.

As mentioned in the first chapter, we will think of our financial lives as a business and we'll call it "HappyLiving Incorporated," or just "HappyLiving," for short. HappyLiving is a company with amazing potential. It is led by an intelligent and motivated person – you! The first, and perhaps most critical move you can make is to establish your mission (your journey's destination). While this may fluctuate and change over time, it is always important to have the end goal in mind when beginning a new journey.

You may already have a sense of what you would like to achieve and accomplish in life. If not, take a moment to relax and imagine your future; imagine that you have lived a full and complete life, have accomplished everything that you wanted, and are reflecting on those achievements. In that moment, what are the most important things to you? Who are the people with you in those moments, and what is the legacy that you will be leaving behind?

Before you go any further with this book, take a moment to try this simple exercise and write down the things that matter the most to you, the things you want to achieve, the people who are important to you, and the legacy that you wish to leave behind. Be as specific and honest with yourself as possible. Formulate those thoughts into a simple statement or short paragraph that can become your life's mission. With that statement in hand, HappyLiving is ready to apply the principles of finance that support successful companies and that will support you as you set out to accomplish great things!

Sanity Check

With all of that visionary, forward-thinking out of the way, let's pull our feet back down to the ground and clarify one very critical point. This book is not a tutorial about how to amass wealth. Quite the contrary, wealth is not the purpose. Money is not what life is about, just as money is not entirely what business is about. For a business, money is the grease that keeps the wheels moving. It is the resource that allows the business to grow. Similarly, your money can be the grease that keeps you moving towards your life's goals and can also be the means for growing your ability to achieve more or widen the influence of the value that you bring. Let's not confuse this with the idea that money can buy happiness or that money is necessary to accomplish great things in life. However, just as a poorly run business stands little chance of reaching its goals, poorly run personal finances can bring misery, heartache, stress, and problems that infect all aspects of life.

The message of this book is not about growing rich. It is about aligning your mission with the financial resources you have in a way that maximizes your satisfaction and sense of purpose; it is about providing you with the knowledge, the vocabulary, and the concepts that can ensure you are *getting the most out of your money.*

Chapter 3

Principle 2:
Mind Your Shareholders

Key Concepts

❖ Companies are owned by shareholders
❖ Investing is a way to give up something of value now for the expectation of greater value in the future
❖ We want to make investments that bring us a return greater than our original investment
❖ Shareholders expect the company to be successful
❖ We have an obligation to protect the long term welfare of the shareholders in our life

Definitions

❖ **stakeholder**   Any person or group with an interest in the business
❖ **share (AKA stock)**   A unit of ownership in a business

- ❖ **shareholder (AKA stockholder)** Any person or entity that owns a share of a business
- ❖ **invest** To give up something now, expecting to receive something of greater value later
- ❖ **investor** A person who invests
- ❖ **return (AKA ROI, Return On Investment)** The value that comes back to an investor from making an investment
- ❖ **dividend** Income received from owning a share
- ❖ **majority shareholder** The person or entity owning more than 50% (majority) of outstanding shares
- ❖ **fiduciary** An individual entrusted with something of value to somebody else
- ❖ **fiduciary responsibility** A relationship of trust between two parties where one party is responsible for the assets of another

In the previous chapter we discussed the "why" behind our journey towards better financial decisions. Our second principle will address the "who" of our financial decisions. With our vision for the future in mind, we must understand *who* will be affected by our plans for the future. We can start this by asking ourselves, "who has an interest in the success of our HappyLiving business?" The second principle, "Mind Your Shareholders" will help anchor and answer that question.

In business, those who have an interest in the company are called **stakeholders**. A stakeholder is any person or group affected by the choices we make. Knowing who our choices affect is important because it helps us stay grounded as we make financial decisions. Great businesses understand all of the groups and parties affected by their decisions and are aware that each financial decision they make will affect one or more of these groups. For a business, these groups include employees, customers, material suppliers, product distributors, government regulators, business partners, and many others. However, among the many groups that businesses take careful consideration of, there is one group which is key to understanding our own HappyLiving business – the **shareholders**. A shareholder is also often called a stockholder (the terms are synonymous).

A shareholder is a person (or any legal entity) that owns a piece of a business (a **share** of the business). A share is a single unit of ownership. We will dive into this concept in greater detail in just a moment. Before we do, there is another important concept that we should explore first; one that will help make sense of our exploration of shares and shareholders. Let's first discuss what it means to **invest**.

Investing

The idea of investing is probably not a new term to most people, but the concepts are important enough to our HappyLiving analogy that it is worth a moment of exploration. To **invest** means to exchange something of value for something else with a higher *expected* value. In other words, you give up something good for something you *expect* to be better. The words *expected* and *expect* are emphasized to imply that there is an element of risk and uncertainty when making an investment in something. It is not the same as a *transaction*, which occurs when we exchange one thing of a known value (money) for something else of a known value (a product). When we invest in something, we are giving away something of known value to us with the expectation that the future will return something even more valuable; by doing so, we become an **investor**.

For example, those of us who have ever paid money for an education, whether for ourselves, a child, or somebody else, might recognize that we were in fact investing in the future of the student. By paying money for tuition and supplies now, as well as *spending time*, we were giving up something of value now expecting to receive something of greater value in the future, such as: a better job, deeper knowledge in a topic of interest, a promotion, or the satisfaction of seeing a loved one excel.

Another example is your decision to purchase and read this book. You are investing both money and time with the expectation of receiving valuable knowledge in return. Hopefully the contents of the book will meet and exceed that expectation!

In essence, we are all investors because we wake up each day with the subconscious notion that we can give up a portion of our lives today in exchange for a brighter future.

The future value that we expect to receive from an investment is called a **return**. This name is appropriate because it represents value that *returns to us* after the investment has been made. This is often referred to as ROI (Return on Investment).

Imagine a boomerang... You throw away something of value with the expectation that it returns to you; but when it returns, you expect it to be bigger, better, and more valuable!

Sometimes, we may not receive a bigger return. In fact, we may receive a return smaller than the original investment or perhaps no return at all. This would be like throwing the boomerang only to see it disappear into the horizon, never to come back. This is where uncertainty and risk come into investing. These two elements, uncertainty and risk, are a natural part of strategic financial management and will be mentioned throughout this book as you prepare your own strategies for finance. As you consider investing your own money, you will always want to reflect on the risks involved before doing so.

Take a Break

Now take a moment to reflect on your HappyLiving business and mission statement. Can you think of a few ways that you can make wise investments now that will lead you to the greater return you are seeking in the future? What will your personal ROI be at the end of your life? Will the investments you make both financially and otherwise be strategically aligned with your personal mission and vision of the future? Are you holding too tightly to your financial boomerang, or perhaps throwing it too far for comfort?

Shareholder

Now that we have discussed what it means to be an investor, we are ready to dive deeper into what it means to be a shareholder.

(Just in case you begin wondering why we are going into such detail here, I assure you that this will all tie into our personal and family financial matters before the end of the chapter!)

A shareholder is a unique type of an investor, so the terms are not synonymous. In other words, all shareholders are investors, but not all investors are shareholders. The investment that a shareholder makes is to exchange something of value now (typically money) in exchange for a share of a business. A share means that the shareholder legally owns a piece of the company. It is like taking the ownership of the company and dividing it into many slices. Each slice represents a share (AKA "stock"). Some people may own a bigger portion of the company, or pie, by holding more shares than others. In general, the more shares you own, the more influence you may have on decisions and the bigger your share will be of any profit that may be distributed.

If you have ever received or bought a share in a company, or if you have a retirement plan that includes shares or stocks of companies, you are literally an owner of those businesses. You are a co-owner with all of the other shareholders. Those companies are responsible to you, as a shareholder (AKA stockholder), to provide a return on your investment – to make money!

So why do shareholders want to own a piece of a company? For a shareholder, owning a share is an investment. That means a shareholder of a business expects to receive a return on that investment. The expected return will come in one or both of two ways: through a **dividend** or through selling the share later at a higher price than what it was purchased for. The latter concept can be illustrated through a simple example. Let's say you buy a share of a company for $1 today and then turn around and sell it for $2 tomorrow. You made money! In fact, if you get a thrill from math you can actually calculate your ROI (Return on Investment) as a percentage, as shown below (for non-math-lovers, just skip over the following equation):

$$ROI = \frac{Return - Cost}{Cost} = \frac{\$2 - \$1}{\$1} = 1.0 \text{ or } 100\%$$

In calculating ROI, anything above 0 is a positive ROI (makes money) and anything below 0 is a negative ROI (loses money). In the case of the $1 share sold for $2, that has a 100% ROI, doubling your money! To translate what ROI is telling us, it simply means that for every dollar invested, you received back your original investment plus an additional X% of that original amount. So for the example above, you received back your dollar plus an additional 100% of that dollar (another dollar). If ROI is negative, it is saying that you received back your original investment, minus X% of the original investment.

The second way that a shareholder receives a return on their investment is through a **dividend** – *income received from owning a share*. When a business earns a profit (i.e. makes money), they will sometimes take some of that money and divide it amongst the shareholders. Essentially, they take their profit and share it with the owners of the company. This dividend then becomes revenue, or income to the shareholder, simply because they own a piece of the company.

To summarize, there are two ways that the shareholder expects to make money: through dividends (when the company shares profits with the shareholders), and through selling the share to somebody else. Both of these methods are tied to one common thing – the performance of the business! If the company does well, the value of the share will go up and the shareholder can sell the share for a higher price. Likewise, if the company does well, they are making money and are more likely to provide a handsome dividend to the shareholders. We can therefore deduce that for the *shareholder* to have a positive ROI (make money), the business must be successful!

The Shareholders in Your Life

With all of that background and financial jargon out of the way, let's get down to business... your business! Let's stop for a moment and think of who might be the shareholders of your HappyLiving business. Who are the people in your life who might "own" a piece of your financial pie? Who holds a share of your financial concerns or rather, who is interested in your financial growth and success? From the perspective of HappyLiving, there are probably no legal shareholders of your finances. However, there are certainly those who invest their time, energy, and emotion hoping to see you succeed. There may be others who depend on your success for their own financial concerns, who depend on you to see their own financial future grow, or whose ROI depends, literally, on your financial performance.

When I think of the shareholders in my life, I think of my immediate family, myself included. Just as most CEOs own a significant number of shares of their company, you, as the CEO of HappyLiving, own a significant number of shares of your business. In fact, you own the majority of HappyLiving's shares, making you the ultimate decision maker and **majority shareholder**. If you have a spouse or partner, then perhaps you both have an equal number of shares of HappyLiving and thus are both interested in seeing your financial situation improve. What about children, siblings, dependent parents, or other close relatives or friends who have a significant interest in your financial well-being? All of these should be counted as shareholders in your life.

As a parent, I consider my children to be among the most important shareholders in my life. Much of their financial future depends on the decisions and financial performance that I deliver today and over the coming years. As I reflect on my finances, I always keep in mind the future of my shareholders and make decisions based on what I believe will provide the best outlook for their future.

I suggest making a list. Writing down the names of your shareholders is a powerful way to realize the impact your financial decisions can have on the future; not only for yourself, but for the others on your list. You may even want to put down the roles of individuals who are perhaps not in your life yet. For example, if you one day plan to marry and/or have children, then you could put these future shareholders on your list as well.

The concept of shareholders is one of the most powerful perspectives that this book can offer to you. As a company makes important financial decisions, they often, if not *always*, have the shareholders at the forefront of their decision making process. Understanding how a decision impacts the long term interest of their shareholders is critical to the success and progress of a company.

As a matter of fact, the relationship between a business and its shareholders is so vital that even the legal system has a say in some of that responsibility. When a person agrees to become the CEO of a corporation, they also become a **fiduciary** for that business. Despite the fancy legal terminology, the concept of being a fiduciary is quite simple; it means that the person has been entrusted with something of value belonging to somebody else. This relationship of trust is called **fiduciary responsibility**. The shareholders of a business are trusting the CEO (among others) to take responsibility for their investment. If the CEO knowingly acts irresponsibly with that investment, or acts outside of the best interest of the shareholders, then not only is that relationship of trust broken, but the shareholders can take legal action against the CEO (having neglected that fiduciary responsibility). This legal protection encourages the CEO to maintain trust and act responsibly with investments.

This is no different for us as individuals. When we make financial decisions, we should ultimately be guided by the shareholders to whom we are responsible. We might consider ourselves as fiduciaries for our loved ones. At the end of each day, it is our shareholders (ourselves included) who will be deeply impacted by our decisions; decisions that have far-reaching impacts throughout all aspects of life and that touch at the very core of our right to experience joy, happiness, and peace of mind.

We should never make financial decisions, particularly major, strategic decisions, without being mindful of the long term welfare of our shareholders (Mind Your Shareholders). As the CEO of HappyLiving, you are the steward responsible for ensuring that your shareholders receive their maximum ROI. This must be done while keeping in mind the important principle we learned from Chapter 1, that *money is only a vehicle for travel, and not the destination.* Know Your Destination. Mind Your Shareholders.

We now have two foundational principles to understanding and managing our personal finances: first, a vision of where we want to be and second, the shareholders who accompany us on our journey. With that platform for success, we are ready to dig deeper into the remaining four principles for making great financial decisions!

Chapter 4

Interlude:
Two *Properties* of Money

M oney is a mysterious thing; we can specify, to the penny, how much money we have, which makes it feel like a very tangible and measurable thing – but this is not true! In fact, this is one of the great misunderstandings that many of us carry around for most, if not all, of our lives. These next two chapters and principles will cover important *properties* of money that can change the way we view our finances. They are: "Time Changes Value", and "Money Seeds Money".

The first, Time Changes Value, is something that affects us on a "macro" scale, or very large scale. It involves how the overall economy of our nation affects our wealth and finances. It is something that we have very little control over – something that *happens to us*.

Conversely, the second, Money Seeds Money, happens on a "micro" scale, or at the individual level. It involves our personal financial situation and how our individual decisions affect our current and future money. This principle is something that we have great control over – it is something that *happens because of us*. Moreover, it is a property of money that can be used to our advantage.

Both of these money-properties are important to understand, as they each have an impact on how we make decisions and derive our financial strategies for success. A knowledge of these two money-properties will provide us with a very strong foundation of understanding and wise decision-making as we apply the tools of business to our HappyLiving endeavors.

Chapter 5

Principle 3:
Time Changes Value

Key Concepts

❖ Money provides a medium for exchanging common values for goods and services
❖ The value of what money can buy changes over time; a dollar today is not the same as a dollar tomorrow

Definitions

❖ **purchasing power** The ability, or power of a dollar to purchase some amount of goods or services
❖ **inflation** When the purchasing power of a dollar decreases over a time period
❖ **deflation** When the purchasing power of a dollar increases over a time period
❖ **projection (AKA forecast)** An attempt to predict the financial outlook of the future

❖ **cash flows** Representation of money flowing in (income) and out (expenses)
❖ **discounting** Method for converting future monetary values to dollars in terms of today's value

Prelude: a Note on Currency

B efore we dive into the next principle, let's explore a little about why money exists at all!

The concept of money has been around for thousands of years. Originally, it developed from some type of precious material (like gold, silver, etc.) that could be commonly valued among people in a village, city, country, and eventually even among inter-state trade. It was a convenient way of spreading economic growth through trade. This made it much easier for merchants to sell their goods and services to others.

Take, for example, a fisherman, a baker, and a net-maker. The fisherman has fish to trade, but needs a new net to catch more fish. The net-maker has nets to trade, but needs a loaf of bread that will pack and carry well for his travels. The baker has bread to trade, but needs fish for his dinner.

Without money, these three merchants are stuck in a dilemma. The fisherman would like to trade fish to the net-maker for a net, but the net-maker doesn't want fish, she wants bread! The baker would love to trade bread to the fisherman for fish, but the fisherman doesn't want bread, he wants a new net!

The solution is simple. Any of the merchants can trade for an item they do not need, but then re-trade that for the item they need. For example, the fisherman can trade fish to the net-maker for a new net and the net-maker can subsequently exchange that fish to the baker for bread, making everybody happy. In the real world, however, such exchanges can become complex and time consuming as merchants run around trying to determine who has what, who needs what, and how to best accomplish the exchanges.

Money is the solution. Rather than trade goods/services for other goods/services, the merchants can instead *sell* their goods or services in exchange for something of common value – money. That money can then be used to purchase goods and services from other merchants who can then continue to circulate that money into the economy by purchasing their own needs and wants.

The Principle

The previous example illustrates an important point; money, by itself, has little to no value. The value lies in the goods and services being purchased, not in the medium for exchanging those goods and services. Money only has value when it can be used to purchase a good or service; and then, the actual worth of that money is not as static (unchanging) as the unwavering numbers printed on the paper would make us believe. The third principle is that "Time Changes Value." In other words, the value of money will change as time ticks away.

If this idea seems difficult to believe, just look at gasoline prices and try the following experiment. Find a $10 bill and calculate how much gas (in gallons) you could purchase today with that $10 (divide 10 by the price per gallon posted at the gas station). Take that $10 bill and tuck it safely away in your wallet, purse, mattress, or other place of safe-keeping. Wait one day. Now pull that $10 bill back out and inspect it. Has it changed at all? Has the number on the bill changed to reflect some new worth? I am going to go out on a limb and guess that you answered "no" to both of those questions. Now check the gas prices at the same gas station you used for pricing previously and re-calculate how much gasoline you can now purchase with that $10. Is the number the same? Repeat this experiment each day for a week. Is the amount of gasoline that you can purchase the same every day? Unless fuel prices have stabilized since this book was published, I would doubt that most people would see the same number calculated each day. I'm sure you see the point and don't really need to waste a week performing that experiment.

Each of us can recognize that the costs of goods and services have changed over the years. We can nostalgically reflect back to the days of our childhood when everything cost less. Has money changed since then? Have all $10 bills changed into $5 bills? Of course not. While dollar bills may not change, the value of goods and services relative to a dollar certainly does. In other words, the quantity of valuable things we can purchase with a dollar is constantly changing. A dollar today is not the same as a dollar yesterday and it will not be the same tomorrow.

This concept is reflected in the term **purchasing power** – the ability, or power, that a dollar has to purchase something of value. When items were *relatively* less expensive back in the 1920's and 1930's, we could say that a dollar in the 1920's had more purchasing power than a dollar today. I cannot buy as much with a dollar today as I could have bought in the 1920's. When purchasing power decreases, such as it has between 1920 and today, that is called **inflation**. So if it feels as though prices for common goods keeps going up, that is inflation.

The opposite of inflation is **deflation** – when the purchasing power of a dollar increases over time. If prices are falling on common goods and services, then this represents deflation.

Here is an analogy that may help explain inflation and deflation. Have you ever had the joy of purchasing a bundle of helium balloons for a party or event? If so, then you know how frustrating it can be to fit those balloons into a vehicle.

Think of the balloons as stuff you can buy (food, home, entertainment, etc.) and the size of those balloons represent the prices of the things you purchase. Your vehicle represents how much money you have to use to purchase stuff. The more the balloons *inflate*, the fewer you can fit into your vehicle; so while the amount of money you have may not change, inflation prevents you from purchasing as much. If you *deflate* the balloons, then you can fit more into your vehicle; again, the amount of money you have has not changed, but because of deflation you can purchase more.

The idea of inflation and deflation illustrates the important notion that the quantity of things we can purchase with our money is always changing; in other words, the value of money changes with time. This is an inherent "economic property" of currency and being aware of this idea will help us understand the landscape of our financial journey.

A Note on Macro-Economics

The causes behind the time value of money are complex interactions that occur throughout our entire nation's economy and increasingly as a result of the global economy. The variables that cause inflation and deflation are beyond the scope of this book. While very interesting and valuable to understand, as individuals, we have very little direct impact on the variables that affect the time value of money. With that in mind, I have opted to only describe how this property affects our individual finances so that we can use this as part of our decision-making foundation. I do, however, encourage all readers to make it a point to learn more about how this money property works on a national and global scale. Such an understanding will help each of us make better decisions in one of the important places that actually can impact what happens on the macro-level: *the voting booth*.

Back to Business

Why is it important to understand this money-property? Businesses use the time value of money in many ways, one of the most important of which is in making financial decisions that affect the longer term outlook of the firm. Warning: financial mumbo-jumbo ahead! When a business is considering an investment, they will do their best to **project** or **forecast the**

cash flows from that investment years into the future and will then **discount** those cash flows back to today's value. *What*!? That's what I asked the first time I heard the term "discounting".

Let's dissect that...

A *projection* or *forecast* (in the financial world) is an analyst's attempt to predict the future. Basically, they are guessing at how much money they think the investment will make or lose over time. Some of the methods out there for this guesswork can be pretty complex and scientific, but in the end, even super-amazing mathematical formulas can't fully predict the future; even still, it is wise to have *some idea* of what the future may (or may not) look like.

Cash flows represent the money that flows in and out of something. Think of a stream of water flowing into a reservoir. As the reservoir fills up, there may be a dam that occasionally lets water flow out. There may be times when the stream has less water flowing into the reservoir, and other times, perhaps after a rainstorm, where the stream is providing substantial water to the reservoir. As time goes on, the amount of water in the reservoir will change. Similarly, in business, the amount of cash the company has will change over time. As income flows into the company and expenses remove cash, the flow of the cash going in and out will change.

Discounting, to most of us, is a way of saving money on a purchase. In the world of finance, however, it is a way of converting the value of a dollar in the future to the value it has today. As the Time Changes Value principle illustrates, the actual value of what a dollar can buy in the future won't match the value it has today. Business folks know this, so they will convert future dollars to *today's value*, a way of ensuring that investment opportunities are being compared "apples to apples."

Putting it all back together now... When a business compares one investment opportunity to another, they want to be sure that all dollars are treated equally, so they convert future money to the value it would have today before doing the comparisons. If you had a choice to accept $1 today or $1 in 10 years, which one of those would have the most value? Which dollar would buy you the most goods? Well, if the economy continues to grow and "inflate," then 10 years from now, a dollar will not be able to buy you as much. So $1 today is more valuable than $1 tomorrow.

Why is this important to us? We don't need to dive into complex math to simply keep in the back of our minds that money will change value over time. We also don't need to worry about discounting cash flows or converting tomorrow's money into today's value. However, we do want to be aware that as we consider our finances, we can store our money or spend our money in various ways. As we make those decisions, we will want to consider the long term implications of the Time Changes Value principle. For example, I can save money by sticking it under my mattress or by putting it in an interest-bearing savings account. Because the value of a dollar is likely to drop over time, the $20 under my mattress won't be able to buy me as much in 10 years as it can now. Putting it in an interest-bearing savings account would be one way to help that money retain more of its value 10 years down the road.

As you consider major financial decisions that will affect your HappyLiving enterprise, always bear in mind the idea that the value of your money will not be the same years from now. Knowing that will help you better understand how the timing of your decisions can impact your finances. Smart businesses always consider the timing of financial decisions; as CEO, so can you, by always remembering that Time Changes Value.

Chapter 6

Principle 4:
Money Seeds Money

Key Concepts

❖ Productivity is at the root of money growth and the heart of the Value Cycle

❖ The Value Cycle takes increased productivity and re-invests it to continue growing

❖ Every dollar has the potential to grow, but requires the right "soil"

❖ Because of compounding, money can grow exponentially

❖ Because of compounding, money can shrink exponentially

❖ The Money Curve provides a map of where we are on our path of financial growth

❖ Paying off debt is an investment in our financial

❖ There are two levers that affect how we move along the Money Curve: Quantity and Interest Rate

Definitions

❖ **compounding** When growth from productivity is used to generate even more growth

❖ **rate of return** The rate (as a percentage) at which money from an investment is returned to you

When introducing Principle 1, Know Your Destination, we explored the idea of money being a resource that can help a business achieve its mission. We discussed how that relates to our personal finances in viewing money as a resource to help us accomplish the things that are truly important to us in life. We discussed money as being the vehicle in our journey, but certainly not the destination.

This concept of using money as a resource for your HappyLiving business is the basis for this chapter and leads to Principle 4, which is that "Money Seeds Money."

When I was a child, I recall taking a handful of pennies and carefully planting them outside in my family's backyard. I watered the pennies and made sure they were planted in an area with good sunlight. I watched day after day for something to sprout, fully expecting that one day I would have a full-grown money tree!

The Next day...

The Next day...

The Next Day...

And the Next day...

It never happened...

Little did I know that money actually *can* plant seeds of growth! Rather than planting that money in the ground and nourishing it with sunlight and earth, I should have planted that money in an investment, nourishing it with knowledge, prudence, and time.

Let's dig deeper...

The Value Cycle

The root of money growth comes from productivity. Money can be used to purchase, harvest, or generate an asset to increase productivity, which then allows for an economy to produce more output given the same inputs. The output then becomes new input, which, given an increase in productivity, then generates even more output.

That was quite a mouthful! Here is a simple way to envision this concept... Put two bunnies in a box and leave them there for a while. Later, you open the box and now you have 10 bunnies; repeat this process with these 10 bunnies and later you might have 100 bunnies; keep repeating this process. I don't recommend that you actually attempt that experiment unless you are particularly fond of bunnies.

1 week later. . .

This type of productivity is what drives economic growth and is what I call the Value Cycle (see Figure 1). Money converts to a productive asset or process, where more value comes out than went in. The extra value is converted back to cash and the process is repeated. Money is not directly causing growth, but it acts as the medium of exchange to purchase, harvest, or generate productive assets that can produce excess growth, which can then be converted back into money.

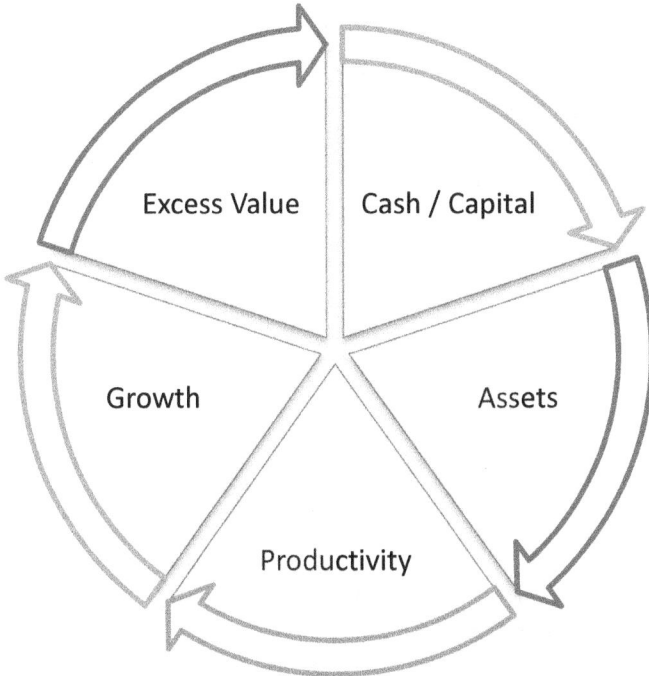

Figure 1. Illustration of the Value Cycle™, © 2013 by Stretto LC (strettoconsulting.com)

This Value Cycle is exactly what great, economic-value-adding companies do: they take some cash, convert it into productivity, which comes back to them as cash, which they convert to even more productivity, which again comes back as cash, etc.

As the HappyLiving business owner, you can do the same thing! You can do this in one of two ways: put your money into an existing Value Cycle, or create your own Value Cycle. In other words, you can take your cash and run your own business or you can put that money into existing businesses or assets as an investment.

As the adage goes, "everything has its opposite." Just as there are two basic ways to grow money, there are two opposing ways to "shrink" it. The first is to do what I did as a child – plant your money in the ground. In other words, you do nothing with it and just hold onto it. Examples of this strategy include: putting money in a safe, under your mattress, or in a buried treasure chest. The second shrink-inducing behavior is spending. Unless you are spending your money on an asset that will bring more money later, money spent is money gone and with it goes the opportunity to invest it into a Value Cycle. This concept is so important it earned its own principle (Spending Closes Doors), which we will explore in great detail in Chapter 9. The following figure illustrates these four ways our money can either grow or shrink.

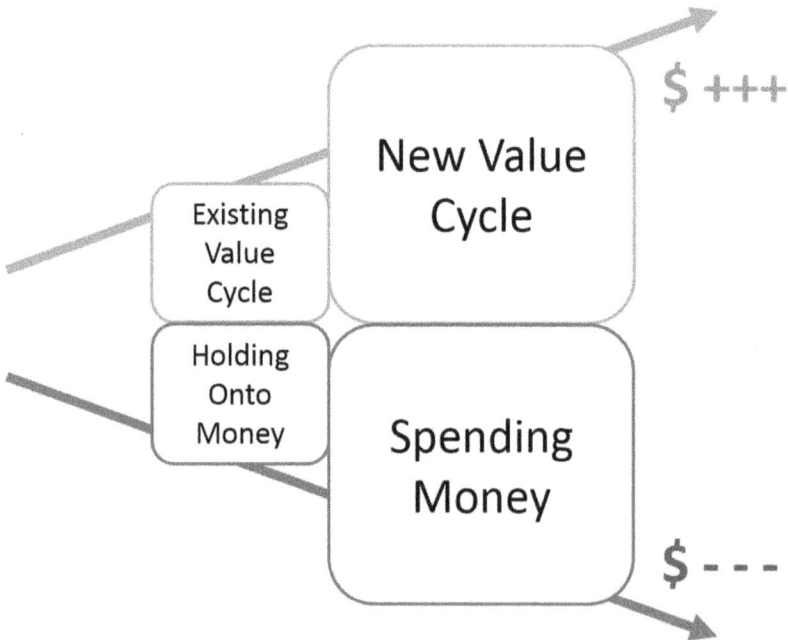

Figure 2. Four ways to grow/shrink money

In reality, most of us end up with some combination of all four. For example, I cannot imagine going a week without enjoying some chocolate-chip cookies. So I might take some cash from my wallet (cash in my wallet is like cash under a mattress – it doesn't grow) and buy myself some nicely processed cookies from my local grocery store. If I am extremely daring, I might use my cash to purchase ingredients to bake my cookies at home. Spending money on cookies does not make me more productive or help me grow my income (only my waistline). So this is like taking money from the "holding on" area and moving it into the "spending" area. At the same time, I might have some money in a savings account (growth from interest), some invested in the stock market (potential growth from investment), and may run a small side business teaching piano lessons on the weekends (converting my productivity and personal knowledge to cash from students). These are each examples of putting money into a Value Cycle. So while it is perfectly normal to have some money flowing in the "shrinking" direction, the key concept here is to try to shift as much as possible to be "growing."

The important thing to understand is that every dollar has the potential to grow, *but only if planted in the right soil.* The right soil is the Value Cycle. You may recall that within the Value Cycle cash can be converted to productivity (producing more output than the required input), creating value that can then be converted back to cash (see Figure 1). Your final cash value will be greater than your initial contribution.

This simple concept is the magic behind business success. A successful business creates a new Value Cycle where the money going in miraculously produces even more coming out! You can apply this principle in your HappyLiving business. As CEO, you are able to make decisions to ensure that your hard-earned money is being invested in a Value Cycle that will provide you with a long-term growth strategy.

Compounding is Wonderful! The Value of Investing

The Value Cycle employs a wondrous mathematical effect known as **compounding** – when growth from productivity is used to create even more growth. This effect is depicted graphically in Figure 3.

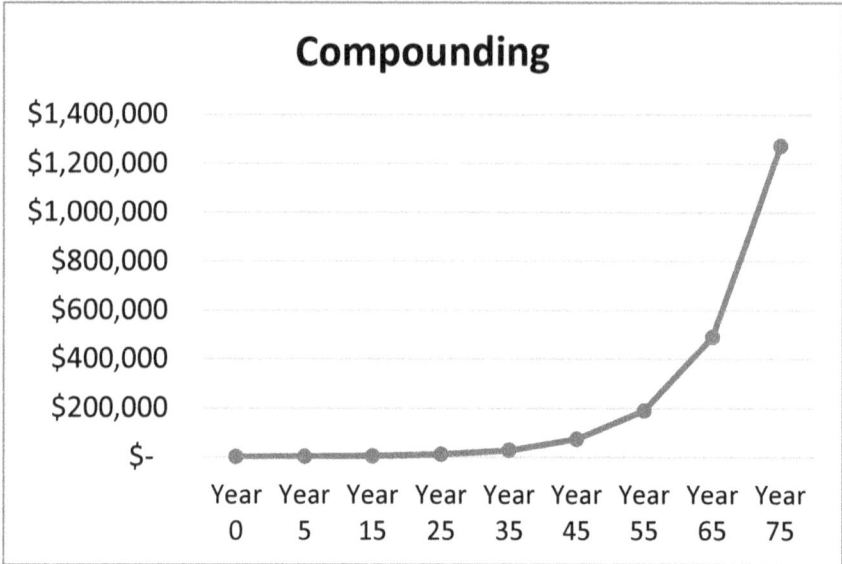

Figure 3. $1,000 compounded annually at 10% over 75 years

The bunny example used when introducing the Value Cycle demonstrates the powerful effect of compounding growth. Now, let's look at a financial example that your HappyLiving business might confront.

Let's assume that you have $1,000 to invest into your retirement. You put that money into a relatively safe investment towards retirement that earns a **rate of return** of 5% per year. After the first year, you will earn $1,000 x 5% = $50.00, so now your retirement account has a balance of $1,050. You will now be earning a return on not just $1,000, but the new balance of $1,050; so the second year return is $1,050 x 5% = $52.50, leaving you with a new balance of $1,050 + $52.50 =

$1,102.50. Figure 4 shows what your balance will look like year after year.

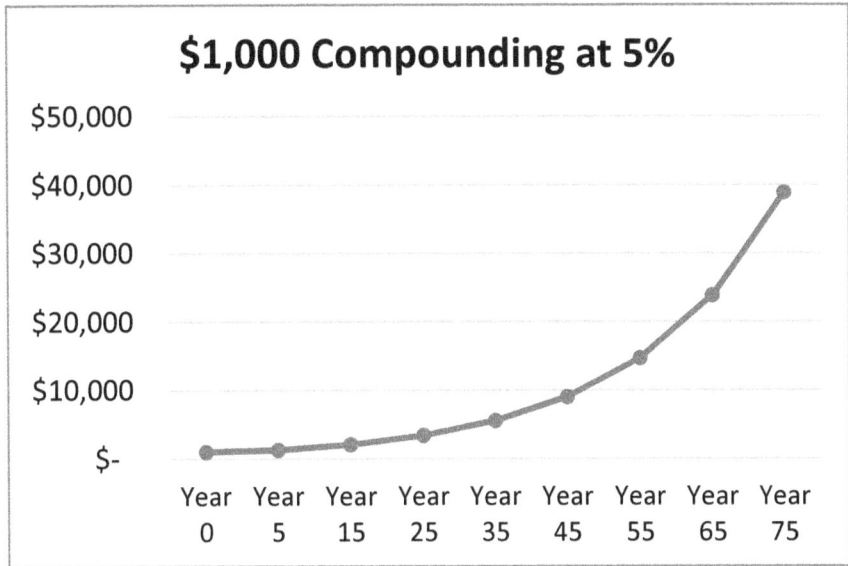

$1,000 Compounding at 5%

Figure 4. Growth effect of 5% annual interest on $1,000 over 75 years

Because of the compounding effect of this investment, after 75 years you will have almost $40,000 (having contributed no more than the original $1,000)! As another example, if you are able to put away $10,000 at 10% growth for 35 years, your final value would be almost $300,000!

These figures illustrate why it is so important to begin saving money towards retirement as early as possible in a person's life or career. While the compounding effect is a wonderful thing, it takes time for its effects to kick in. Putting money away towards retirement in an investment with a compounding effect is a very real application of the old saying, "good things come to those who wait."

Compounding is Terrible! The Crisis of Debt

Newton's third law of physics states, "for every action, there is an equal and opposite reaction." This isn't a book on physics, but Newton's law has great application in understanding how compounding can also suck the money right out of your pocket – through debt.

There are many types of debt out there, but some of the most dangerous ones are those that take advantage of the compounding effect. We just demonstrated that compounding can make a person quite wealthy over time; but if you are on the giving side of that money, rather than the receiving side, then that same wealth-building mathematical wonder will be taking wealth out of your pocket with increasing speed to line the pockets of those to whom you are indebted. Lenders have known about the compounding effect of money for a long time. The figure demonstrating compounding (Figure 3) works exactly the same for lenders. Unfortunately for us (the consumers), it means our chart is flipped upside down, as shown in Figure 5.

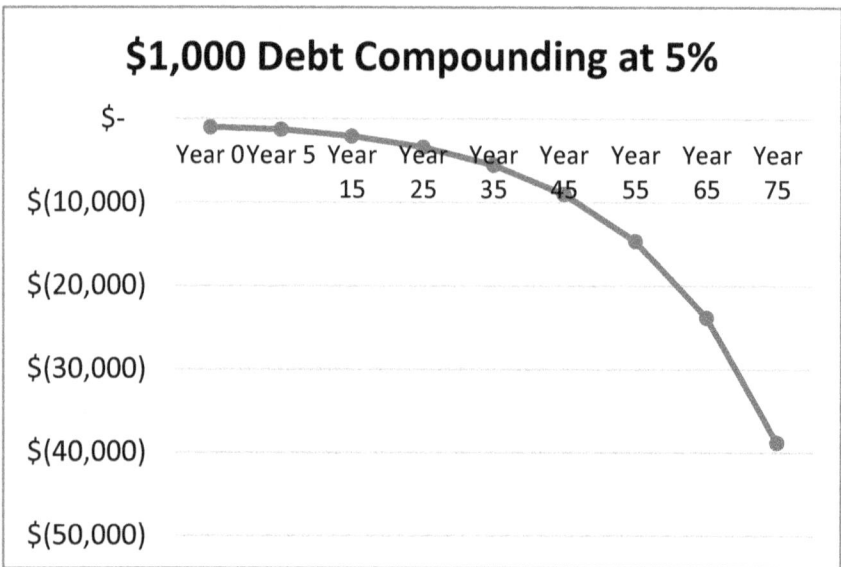

Figure 5. Debt effect of 5% annual interest on $1,000 over 75 years

If you have ever been in debt and felt as though you were "drowning" or that there appeared to be no way to get out of debt, you are probably experiencing the negative effects of compounding. It is a horrible feeling and one that we will shortly attempt to address. But first, we need to fully understand the financial situation that compounding debt puts us into.

When we were looking at the compounding effect from an investment standpoint, we saw that it takes quite a while for this affect to really kick in; so why does it seem like the compounding effect of debt happens so much more quickly? It feels that way, because *it is that way*. To speed up the effect of compounding, lenders just need to raise the interest rate. Doing so shortens the time it takes for that compounding affect to apply in a very dramatic way.

Compare the two lines in Figure 6. One demonstrates the compounding affect at a 5% interest rate while the other shows the compounding affect at a 25% interest rate. Look at how much faster a higher interest rate will bring on a personal financial crisis! At 5%, the debt has hardly begun to curve after 5 years; but at 25%, the debt has already more than tripled after the same time.

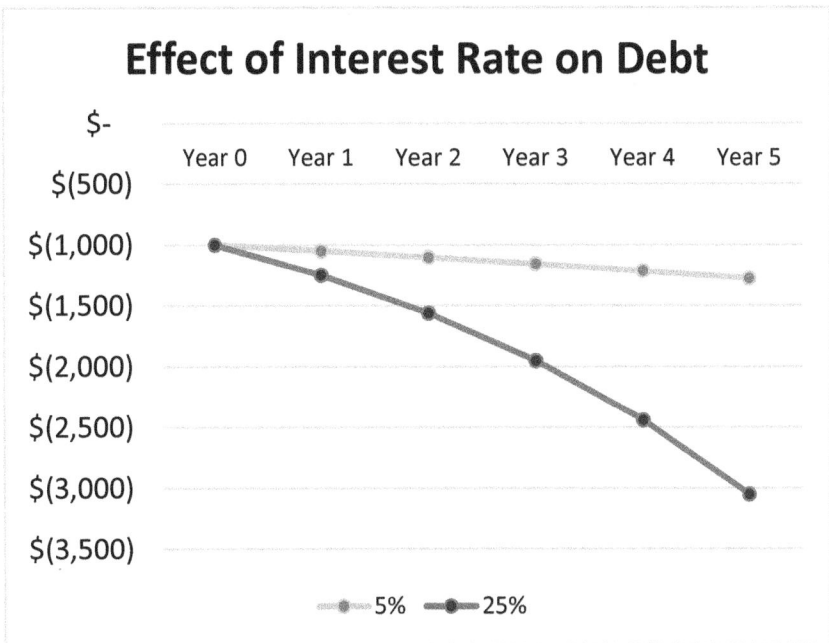

Effect of Interest Rate on Debt

Figure 6. Effect of 5% vs. 25% annual interest rate on $1,000 debt over 5 years

The higher the interest rate, the shorter the time it takes to reach a financial crisis.

Changing Perspectives and Investing in You

Now let's take a moment to reflect on our own financial situation. Does your personal finance curve look like the positive, value-generating graph we first became excited over (Figure 4), or does it more closely resemble the negative, value-destroying graph that brings a feeling of helplessness (Figure 5)?

Whatever your situation, just think of it as a point on a journey. We can depict this journey graphically by combining our two compounding curves (Figure 4 & Figure 5). We will then flip the debt curve around to indicate our readiness to reverse the trend and head in the right direction. Let's call this the Money Curve (Figure 7).

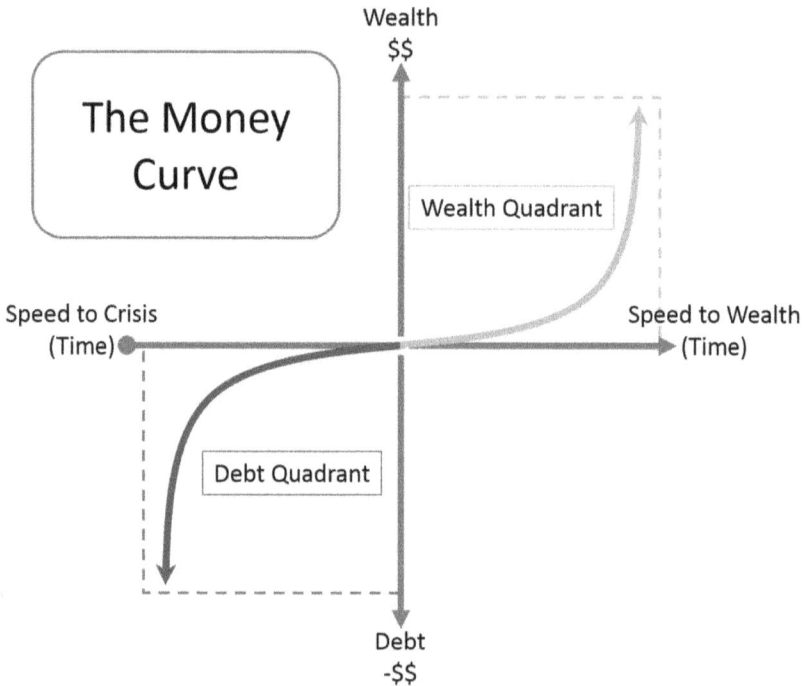

Figure 7. The Money Curve, © 2013 by Stretto LC (strettoconsulting.com)

This represents a financial journey over time. The destination is the same for all of us, although we may differ in where we are currently positioned along the journey. If you are below the positive line in the *debt quadrant* (lower left), be confident that as you pay off those debts (and prevent yourself from taking on new debts), you are moving back along the path towards the *wealth quadrant.* So paying off those debts should not feel like throwing money away; rather, you are investing in yourself to move towards your financial goals. Again, just be careful to not take on new debts, as those will just pull you back down to the left.

If you are in the wealth quadrant (top right), then you are actively investing in your future and are progressing towards the far right. This is a great place to be. As you progress towards the top-right of the wealth quadrant, you will feel more empowered and independent.

I encourage you to take some time to reflect on where you are along the curve. Even a "gut feel" will help you to understand your current position and guide you towards the next steps necessary to continue your progress. Regardless of where you find yourself along the Money Curve, you can always find a way to move further along the path of the wealth quadrant!

How can we change our position on the curve? There are two levers you can pull to control both your speed and position along the path. First, is the interest rate, second is the quantity.

Interest Rate Lever

This may be mostly out of your control, but an understanding of how the interest rate affects your speed will help you make wise decisions for your HappyLiving business. The interest rate controls the length of time it takes for the compounding affect to kick in. On the Money Curve, this is represented on the horizontal arrow labeled "Time". The higher the interest rate, the more quickly you will move along that horizontal line. From an investment perspective, this means that the higher your rate of return on your investments, the more quickly you will reach the wealth waiting on the right side of the curve. From a debt perspective, it means the higher the interest rate of the debt, the more quickly you will reach the financial crisis waiting on the left side of the curve.

Quantity Lever

This lever affects the total scale of the vertical arrows labeled with "$$". The more money you put into investments, the higher the wealth end of the Money Curve will climb; conversely, the more money you use from debt, the deeper the financial crisis will become.

In summary, the Interest Rate Lever affects how fast we are moving towards crisis or wealth. The Quantity Lever affects how big the numbers are. In other words, it affects the amount of wealth potentially building on the far right or the amount of debt potentially deepening at the far left.

None of us can perfectly control these two levers, but we can certainly influence them to some degree. Let's look at an example. Say we just received a pay check. After meeting all of our obligations, we have $100 left over that does not need to be reserved for any upcoming expense. First, we identify which quadrant we are in: the wealth quadrant or the debt quadrant? If the answer is "the wealth quadrant", we then pull on the Quantity Lever and decide how much of that $100 we want to put into future wealth vs. current spending. Remembering the compounding affect and remembering that putting in more money now potentially means much bigger numbers later, our HappyLiving shareholders may someday thank us for choosing to invest all $100.

What about the Interest Rate Lever? We pull this lever when we choose where or how to invest those excess funds. We may not control the interest rates of our investment options, but we do have choice over the investment options themselves. These options may include things such as: personal savings, mutual funds, stock market, certificate of deposit, 401K, IRA, etc. We use our best judgment to determine where we think our money will best serve the purpose of shortening the horizontal axis (time) of the Money Curve, bringing our HappyLiving business closer to wealth more quickly.

Now what if we find ourselves in the debt quadrant? We can pull those same two levers. First, we pull the Quantity Lever and choose how much of that $100 we should *invest* in paying off our debts, remembering that the more money we invest in paying off debts, the more shallow that financial crisis becomes (shortening the vertical axis of the Money Curve). Wisely, we may choose to put all $100 towards debts, understanding that it moves us further away from the debt quadrant and closer to the wealth quadrant.

The Interest Rate Lever can then be pulled by selecting which of our debts to put this money towards. This choice should be made (after all minimum payments have been met), based primarily on the interest rate of the loan/debt. Recalling that higher interest rates translate to a longer road to get out of debt, we will want to put this $100 into the debt with the highest interest rate. This propels us forward towards the wealth quadrant by reversing the compounding affect that the financial institutions rely on to pull money out of our pocket. In other words, it shortens the horizontal axis of the Money Curve, making our journey out of the debt quadrant and into the wealth quadrant move more rapidly.

Does the Money Curve perspective work for everybody? I believe it does. Some people may never experience the loss that comes with excessive debt, and some may never experience the freedom of complete financial control and growth; but I believe the *opportunity* to live on the far-right side of the Money Curve is there for everybody. The pathway is there; it is simply a matter of understanding your current position on that path and then choosing and committing to make the changes necessary to move forward. With time, patience, knowledge, and confident action, I believe that anybody can progress from any point on the curve towards the far-right end where financial control and freedom are waiting.

Chapter 7

Interlude:
Two *Perspectives* on Money

While the previous two chapters and principles covered very important *properties* of money, these next two chapters and principles will cover important *perspectives* about money. By combining a solid understanding of the fundamental properties of our money with the appropriate perspectives for growing our HappyLiving business, we will end up with a successful, lifelong model for financial progress! The two perspectives are: "See Tomorrow, Today" and "Spending Closes Doors".

The first, See Tomorrow, Today, will provide us with a long-term perspective; one that will help keep us on the proverbial road towards our destination. One of the biggest challenges in proper financial management is to keep one eye on the end goal, rather than focus entirely on the present.

The second, Spending Closes Doors, will provide us with a broader short-term perspective of how our financial habits and behaviors affect us both immediately and in the long term. In this sense, this second perspective of money will broaden the vision of our financial landscape.

These two financial perspectives are fundamental to successful business growth in modern economies. HappyLiving can similarly benefit from the ability to better comprehend the breadth and depth of our financial decisions.

Chapter 8

Principle 5:
See Tomorrow, Today

Key Concepts

❖ Lifespans are increasing, which results in increasing costs for retirement (living longer requires more money)

❖ Most of the U.S. is not on track to have adequate funds for retirement

❖ Saving money now for our retirement is critical to the success of our HappyLiving business and for the welfare of its shareholders

---

Why are longer lifespans killing us? This chapter will answer that question while exploring the fifth principle – See Tomorrow, Today.

Allow me to play the role of artist for a moment and paint a picture of the average U.S. citizen's future. Before I start to lay out the brush strokes, it is important to note that the analytical exercise we are about to engage in is based on data that is averaged for U.S. citizens. That means it is almost guaranteed to be precisely wrong! Your situation may be better or worse than the picture we will soon paint; but without being able to predict the future, using averages will at least give us some idea of what might lay ahead.

I will lay the groundwork for our predictive artwork by first telling the true tale of the demise (I use that term loosely) of a large corporation – GM (General Motors).

Employing over 200,000 people during its peak, GM produced and sold millions of cars throughout the world. By number of sales, GM has always been ranked among the top automakers. In fact, for the vast majority of GM's sales history, they were ranked #1, worldwide.

In 2009, GM filed for Chapter 11 bankruptcy. As a result, GM was "reorganized." That is a nice way of saying that the company's financial structure, as well as its product lines and brands, were pulled apart, gutted, and re-evaluated.

This begs the question, why would the world's top automaker need to file for Chapter 11 bankruptcy? What led to this horrible financial situation? There is no easy answer to this question and many theories abound. However, the data that we can pull from GM's public financial records point to some interesting, thought-provoking, and, in many ways, frightening answers.

When GM filed their financial reports for the year 2008, they reported that between the years 2006 and 2008 they recorded combined expenses of more than $25,000,000,000 (25 BILLION dollars) related to pension and retirement benefits!

Having an 11-digit expense is something that any modern company would not take lightly, as that is a mighty large check to write! (Visit www.sec.gov for financial information on GM and other publicly-traded companies.)

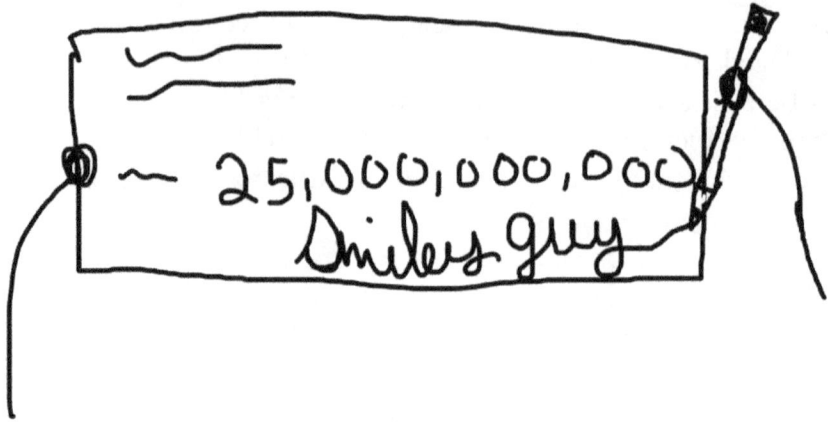

GM certainly took notice and aggressively worked to restructure their pension plans and retirement benefits over this period as well as the years following. One might infer that GM simply could not afford the pension and retirement benefits that they had agreed to pay to their employees; but how could such a thing happen? How would a company so large and powerful miscalculate their ability to pay out on retirement benefits?

I propose that the trouble really started brewing back in the 70s and 80s. During this time, pension plans were quite popular in the U.S. (no longer the case). In exchange for employee loyalty, these plans would offer the employee benefits after they had served to retirement age and those benefits would typically extend until the end of that person's life.

And therein lies the problem... "until the end of ... life." Retirement benefits cost companies money, and if these benefits are paid out until the retiree dies, these costs are directly related to the lifespan of the retirees.

Let's hold that thought about GM's retirement benefits for a moment and explore a bit more about lifespans (we'll tie the two together shortly). The WHO (World Health Organization) collects and analyzes data related to human health, including the creation of life expectancy tables. If you have ever heard somebody speak about life expectancy or average lifespans, this data likely came from the WHO. The information is updated every few years based on actual mortality rates.

Back in the 70s and 80s, when many of these pension plans were being designed and created, the WHO reported the average life expectancy for U.S. citizens to be 67 for men and 75 for women (visit www.census.gov for additional life expectancy information). Most people planned to retire at the age of about 65. As the majority of workers with retirement benefits at this time were male, this required GM to provide about 2 years of benefits for most of their employees.

Over the last several decades, due to better health care and healthier living, the average life expectancy has changed. The life expectancy in 2008 was recorded at about 81 for women and 76 for men. That is almost a decade added onto the life of the average U.S. male and approximately 6 years for the average U.S. female! Additionally, more females have entered the workforce, raising the retiree average lifespan even more as a result of the generally longer lifespans for female retirees.

So back to GM, how does that ever-increasing lifespan affect GM's retirement benefits? Let's assume they previously planned on providing $20,000 of post-retirement benefits per individual (I arbitrarily picked that number). Originally, they may have calculated that they would need two years times $20,000 = $40,000 per employee, on average. Now, they would need to plan on 10 years times $20,000 = $200,000 per employee. That is a 500% increase in the cost of providing post-retirement benefits! Multiply that by tens of thousands of employees, and it is no wonder why GM recorded an 11-digit retirement expense.

This revelation also helps explain why most modern companies no longer offer pension-type plans. Instead, they prefer to contribute towards their employee's individual retirement plans, such as a 401K. This allows the company to contribute towards a person's retirement as a benefit without taking any risk based on the actual lifespan of the employee. In essence, the responsibility for ensuring we have enough money for retirement has shifted from the business to the individual. Businesses may contribute towards retirement, but it is up to us, as individuals, to ensure that the amount we have saved for our retirement is adequate.

Now back to our painting of the future. So how much do we need to have for our retirement? Let's use very broad brush strokes to paint this picture by eliminating complex factors such as inflation or deflation, sale of assets, etc. We'll also use the data provided by U.S. averages to keep things simple.

To figure out how much we might need for retirement, we just need to take the number of years we plan on being in retirement and multiply that by how much we think it will cost us to live during each year of retirement. Going back to our averages, the average life expectancy for all U.S. citizens (male or female) is projected to be about 80 years. Most people I talk to still think of 65 as being a good retirement age. Therefore, if we plan to be in retirement for about 15 years, that means we should plan on living for about 15 years without any income.

According to the U.S. Census Bureau, the U.S. median household income between the years 2006-2010 was just below $52,000 per year. Ignoring inflation and making nice round numbers, let's assume we will want to have about $50,000 per year to maintain our average standard of living. Keep in mind that health care for the elderly can be very expensive and is not reflected in this number (we are ignoring many details).

Based on those numbers, to maintain an average standard of living during a retirement of 15 years, we will need to have 15 times $50,000 = $750,000 in our retirement funds. Now go check your retirement account. How are you doing? Are you on track? Well, we can calculate that pretty easily by taking the total we need and dividing it by the number of years we have until we retire to see just how much we need to be saving each year.

If you are currently about 30 years old, then you have 35 years to save $750,000 for retirement, or $750,000 / 35 = **$21,429 per year**. If you are currently about 40 years old, then you have 25 years to save $750,000 for retirement, or $750,000 / 25 = **$30,000 per year**.

These simplified examples ignored two of our key principles: Time Changes Value and Money Seeds Money. The first affects the inflation rate and purchasing power of each dollar we invest (see Chapter 5 for review). The second affects the rate at which each dollar we invest can grow (see Chapter 6 for review). Both of these can dramatically alter the outcome of our financial planning and efforts. (The math used to calculate the following example is a bit complex, so I've left out the step-by-step details for simplicity.)

Let's re-calculate the case of the 30 year old wanting to save $750,000 for retirement. We'll use an estimated inflation rate of 3% and a moderate annual investment return of 8% (not your typical savings account), and we'll even account for good-old Uncle Sam (capital gains tax rate of 15%, the current tax rate for long-term investment returns). Understanding the impact of the Time Changes Value principle and taking advantage of the Money Seeds Money principle now requires an investment of only (imagine number-crunching here) **$7,600 per year**! That annual contribution would need to be adjusted each year to account for inflation (3% more per year), but is almost one third the amount we would need if we did not take advantage of the Money Seeds Money principle! Understanding how to *grow* money versus simply *saving* money is well worth our time.

Depending on your age and how you choose to invest your money, every situation will be different; but how are you feeling about your situation? Are you on track? I hope that you are! Based on U.S. averages, sadly, most of us are not. According to the EBRI (Employee Benefit Research Institute, www.ebri.org), fewer than 60% of people are saving towards their retirement. Among those who are saving, about 60% report that their total retirement funds are less than $25,000; 30% have less than $1,000! Only 10% of those in the survey have more than $250,000 in their retirement savings/investment plan.

It is also important to note that those who have calculated their own retirement needs, based on personalized data and goals, frequently calculate a need for more than $1 million in their retirement plan. So our initial number of $750,000 is likely too low for many of us. Again, this analysis was greatly simplified. Consider speaking with a professional finance advisor to determine a more accurate image of what your needs may be for retirement.

This paints a fairly bleak picture. Most of us are not going to be able to afford our own retirement. The fact that we live longer requires more money to support our standard of living for that duration, and the sad fact is there are few who are adequately preparing for the future.

How do we solve this problem? How can we change the painting of our future to convey a more pleasant image? Just as we discussed having two "levers" to pull back in the chapter on Principle 5, our ability to adequately save for retirement is also affected by two levers that we can control. The first lever is the length of retirement and the second is the amount we save towards our retirement plan. Similar to Principle 5, these levers deal with time and quantity.

Time Lever: Length of Retirement

Shortening our retirement will require less money to support that retirement (pretty simple). We can shorten our retirement in two ways: retire later or die earlier. All of us want to live longer, so we won't even explore the latter option. That leaves us with "retire later."

Based on informal surveying and discussions with many people, I've learned that planning on working until the age of 75 or 80 is an increasingly popular option. It is pretty easy to project a solution such as this onto our future selves. If you might be considering this as an option, let me offer three insights that might make you reconsider the idea of working longer as a "retirement plan".

First, our physical and mental faculties deteriorate over time. Our ability to work and stay in the labor force reduces with age. Our ability to contribute in a productive and meaningful manner will wane as the years go by. Relying on a future self, who is likely to be less competent than our current self, comes with great risk.

Second, we are constantly receiving an influx of new entrants into the workforce; namely, the children of the current generation and future generations. If we are still in the workforce as these generations progress, we will be directly competing for jobs.

From an employer's perspective, would a business rather have an up-and-coming, ambitious, energetic, and productive entrant, or a 75-80 year old worker? Pause and give this serious reflection. This is precisely the choice hiring managers will be making in the coming decades and is one that may affect your retirement plan. Especially if that plan includes staying in the work force until you are 80 (or even 70)!

Third, and last, some research indicates that an employer's costs for elderly employees are higher than those of younger, healthier employees. This is yet another reason why employers might hesitate to choose the more experienced (but much older) 80-year old over the less experienced (but younger and less costly) 30-year old.

Working past the 70-year mark is certainly a possibility, but comes with great risks. Our retirement plans should prepare us accordingly. As you consider the possibility of working through your elderly years, reflect back on your personal mission and vision. In particular, bear in mind the effect this decision will have on your future self and your HappyLiving shareholders (Mind Your Shareholders – see Chapter 3).

Quantity Lever: Amount of Retirement Savings

This lever is conceptually very simple. If you can possibly squeeze more money into your retirement plan now, do it! There is an old saying that "the best time to plant a tree is 20 years ago. The second best time is now!" That is so true of our retirement future. We should have started saving long ago for our future, but if we haven't, the second best time to start putting funds away is now!

Recalling principle 4, Money Seeds Money, may help encourage you to put away as much as you reasonably can into a Value Cycle for growth. This may be a good time to review that principle (Chapter 6). Understanding how money can multiply will ease some of the burden that retirement pressure places on our backs while inspiring us to continue progressing along the Money Curve.

Saving for retirement is critical for your HappyLiving business and its shareholders! That statement summarizes it all. Take the time to review your financial situation, your goals, and your mission. Think about how your financial actions now will affect your ability to act in the future. Look ahead. Plan ahead. See Tomorrow, Today.

Chapter 9

Principle 6:
Spending Closes Doors

Key Concepts

- ❖ When we spend money, we are also making a choice not to spend or invest that money on something else
- ❖ The price of something is not a true reflection of its actual value
- ❖ Spending money now costs us the opportunity for that money to grow into the future

Definitions

- ❖ **opportunity cost**   The foregone value of the next best alternative when making a decision
- ❖ **utility**   The economical term for the "happiness" factor, satisfaction, or pleasure that comes from something

O ur last, and perhaps most influential business principles is that Spending Closes Doors. The concepts discussed here can be used in business, personal finance, and virtually any other aspect of life that requires decision-making. This principle will help us understand the choices placed in front of us more fully, guiding us in choosing the best option. The business term for this is **opportunity cost**.

Opportunity cost is the foregone value of the next best alternative to a decision. Intuitively, it is what you are giving up when you choose one opportunity over another. When it comes to finances, whenever you choose to spend or allocate money in one way, you are also choosing (consciously or otherwise) what *not* to spend or invest those funds on. This is critical for businesses to understand, as they are often faced with a variety of ways to spend business funds. Likewise, our HappyLiving business faces multiple options on what to do with money.

Perhaps this is best illustrated with a story... I was first introduced to the concept of opportunity cost by my father when I was a young man. I had saved my money for months so that I could purchase an Iguana (a relatively expensive pet lizard). I had about $40 saved up and was anxious to bring my new pet home.

After driving me to the pet store, my dad paused before going inside. "Are you sure you want to spend all of your money on a lizard?" he questioned.

"Of Course!" I replied.

"But just think about what you could do with that money! You could buy 40 milk shakes or 80 candy bars!" my dad protested.

I gave this only a moment's thought before replying that I was determined to buy an Iguana; and so I did. The poor creature died three weeks later, apparently ill before I had even made the purchase.

Without using the terminology, my dad was teaching me about opportunity cost. When we make a decision to do one thing, there is an opportunity cost equal to the value of the next best thing. By choosing to buy an Iguana, I had an opportunity cost equal to 40 milk shakes or 80 candy bars! The cost of that Iguana went beyond just the $40 in my wallet; it extended to all of the happiness and pleasure I could have obtained through the purchase of something else, like 40 milkshakes! My dad was trying to show me that maybe the Iguana wouldn't bring me as much "happiness value" as the same money spent on something else. Ultimately, he was right.

In economics, the idea of non-monetary or non-dollar value is called **utility**. The *utility* of something indicates the satisfaction, happiness, or pleasure that somebody would derive from something. In the case of my Iguana, I thought that the utility of spending $40 on a lizard would bring me years of happiness from caring for a pet. The thought of that companionship seemed to outweigh the fleeting happiness of downing 40 milkshakes… but as the saying goes, "hindsight is 20/20!" So the *opportunity cost* was not just $40, but actually $40 *plus* the opportunity to have gained more happiness (utility) from something else. *The price of something is not a true reflection of its actual value.*

Remember, whenever you choose to spend a dollar, you are also making a choice on what *not* to do with that dollar. How many of us pause to reflect on what we are choosing *not* to do with our money? Well, it is about time that we give it a try. It might be surprising how often we end up choosing lower-utility (shorter-term happiness) opportunities with our money!

Let's make sure our HappyLiving CEO hat is on now. Opportunity cost is very important to business. A modern company evaluates prospective projects or uses of resources against their opportunity cost. They do this by asking the simple question of what they could do otherwise with that resource. For example, if an employee proposes a new idea that will cost $1,000,000, the company will look at what alternatives they have for using those million dollars. If no better opportunities present themselves, or rather, if there is no opportunity with a higher ROI, then they may choose to go forward with the employee's proposed project. The opportunity cost of that project would be the next best alternative that was NOT chosen.

Let's use an example to further illustrate how this plays out in business. We'll use a fictitious company called ThrivingBusiness. ThrivingBusiness has $100,000 that they would like to spend on a new project and they invite the employees to submit ideas. An employee, we'll call her Alice, has an idea to buy new software that will increase employee performance, resulting in a savings of $50,000 per year. Another employee, Bob, submits an idea to spend the money on new office chairs, which will improve employee satisfaction, resulting in an estimated productivity boost worth $40,000 per year. Both *opportunities* cost $100,000 and both will end up saving the company money year after year. So which does ThrivingBusiness choose? They do not have a large enough budget to do both, so they will choose the opportunity with the greatest overall value. Fortunately for Alice, that means her idea is the winner, as each year the new software will save the company $10,000 more than the new office chairs would save in increased productivity ($50,000 per year - $40,000 per year = $10,000 per year).

The opportunity cost of Alice's proposal is the $40,000 per year that could have been saved from Bob's idea; but the opportunity cost of Bob's idea was the $50,000 per year that could be saved from Alice's proposal.

This is an important concept for our HappyLiving business. As it turns out, sometimes the opportunity cost of a decision to spend money ends up being bigger than the value of what we paid! In such a case, it means we made an unwise decision by spending money on something that wasn't really worth its true cost.

As it turns out, keeping an Iguana for only three weeks was not worth more to me than 40 milkshakes! If I had been able to predict the future, I would have made a different choice. Our financial decisions often do not have such immediate repercussions. In fact, we may not truly see the impact of our financial choices until much later in life. As a result, it is hard for us to understand the true cost of spending money.

This is particularly true when looking towards our future retirement, or perhaps future savings goals (like a child's educational expenses, a dream vacation, a new home, etc.) Every time we spend a dollar, the cost of whatever we are buying is actually *greater than the dollar being spent*. This is because each dollar has *earning potential* and has the ability to grow money now and into the future. When we spend it, we lose that opportunity. I recently came across this paragraph by Benjamin Franklin from his work titled, *Advice to a Young Tradesman, Written by an Old One* (1748):

> *'Money can beget money, and its offspring can beget more, and so on. Five shillings turned is six, turned again is seven and threepence, and so on, till it becomes a hundred pounds. The more there is of it, the more it produces every turning, so that the profits rise quicker*

and quicker. He that kills a breeding sow, destroys all her offspring to the thousandth generation. He that murders a crown, destroys all that it might have produced, even scores of pounds."

In this somewhat graphic reference of murdering money, Benjamin Franklin summarizes the idea of opportunity cost. If we "murder" a dollar by spending it, we have also "murdered" the future money that would have grown from that dollar.

This concept can't be emphasized enough and I strongly recommend that before making any purchase, no matter how insignificant it may seem, we give serious consideration to what we are giving up in the future to obtain something now. HappyLiving should thrive by deliberate choice in how money is being spent and how it is *not being spent.*

In a recent conversation with a friend who was struggling with some financial decisions, we began talking about some spending habits and the idea of opportunity cost. After making some quick-and-dirty calculations, we were able to determine that buying that new pair of pants at Nordstrom's, however fashionable, was just like taking an entire course out of her son's future college education.

Can you imagine if such an analogy were real? Would you ever recommend that a person sacrifice one course from their child's education to pay for a fashionable pair of jeans?

While it may seem to be a stretch of reality, I propose that it is real – very real indeed! At some point in the future, we might find ourselves wishing that we had a little more income to pay for that child's education, a replacement for a leaky roof, a new transmission for a broken down car, a hip surgery, or a plethora of other expenses that may await us in the future. The fact is, when we spend money today, we are spending more than just the value of that money; we are also spending the potential future value of that money, which is much larger than we may realize. If you need a bit more convincing on the future value of money, this may be a good point to go back and review principle 4 – Money Seeds Money!

So what should we do now with this added perspective that Spending Closes Doors? Answer: we use it to make better decisions! To guide our spending it would be helpful to know the true cost of the things we are spending our money on. Corporations use fancy mathematical algorithms to help estimate values and opportunity costs. HappyLiving may not have such elaborate tools, but here is a "rule of thumb" that I'll propose to simplify "true cost" calculations: multiply each dollar by the rough number of decades between now and your savings goal and then double that number.

For example, if you have a dream of buying a beachside condo in about 10 years and you are about to spend $500 on a new video game console, first, multiply the $500 by the rough or rounded number of decades:

$500 x 1 = $500

Next, double that number:
$500 x 2 = **$1,000**

Based on our rule of thumb, that $500 is really closer to $1,000! Imagine taking $1,000 away from your ability to set money aside for that condo; or perhaps you can imagine the price of that condo going up by another $1,000.

Now let's look at a retirement example… let's say I am *about* 3 decades away from retirement. I just received my tax refund and am thinking of spending $1,000 on a new home theater set. How might this affect my retirement? First, multiply by the approximate number of decades:

$1,000 x 3 = $3,000

Next, double that number:
$3,000 x 2 = **$6,000**

$6,000 could go a long way in those retirement years! Perhaps I should stick with my current entertainment set a little longer…

Spending money now closes doors of opportunity that cannot be opened again with those same funds. Spending money in certain ways can also open doors of opportunity (e.g. investments), in which case, the question becomes "which door of opportunity is best to open?" As we make spending decisions, we should always be aware that other doors of opportunity will close.

At the very least, before spending your hard-earned cash, pause and reflect on the Money Seeds Money principle. These two principles combined (Money Seeds Money and Spending Closes Doors) can guide are spending and saving habits towards wiser paths. The good (and sometimes not-so-good) folks in the financial industry can sure build a lot of complexity around how to use opportunity cost in decision-making. For HappyLiving, however, it is quite simple... just remember that when you spend money, you are also choosing not to spend that money on something else. Spending Closes Doors.

Chapter 10

Review and Conclusion

L et's review some of what we have accomplished!

- ❖ We have created and reflected on our life's mission and vision
- ❖ We have identified the shareholders who share in our HappyLiving business venture
- ❖ We have explored two important *properties* of money that will provide a solid foundation for financial decision-making
- ❖ We have discussed two key *perspectives* of money that will guide our values and strategies as we make critical financial decisions

In other words, we have stepped back to look at our financial situation and future to identify these important parts:

- ❖ Where we would like to be and where we are going
- ❖ Who is important to us in our journey
- ❖ What mechanisms can help us reach our destination
- ❖ What road blocks may exist along the way

❖ How we can alter our perspectives to guide us along our financial travels

A business can be more successful in accomplishing its mission through proper financial management and the six principles outlined in this book are fundamental to that success. Likewise, we can be successful in accomplishing our vision for HappyLiving by applying the same concepts. We should regularly review the concepts and principles in this book to make them a natural part of our financial language, thoughts, and ultimately our decisions! We can feel confident in our ability to provide a great future for our HappyLiving business and a wonderful *return on investment* for our shareholders!

---

6 Business Principles to Advance Your Personal Finances

1 Know Your Destination
2 Mind Your Shareholders
3 Time Changes Value
4 Money Seeds Money
5 See Tomorrow, Today
6 Spending Closes Doors

Acknowledgements

Writing a book comes with many challenges and requires the support and endurance of multiple individuals. I thank the businesses which, over the years, have contributed to my personal experiences and the personal knowledge upon which the contents of this book stemmed. Likewise, my gratitude goes out to friends and family who have helped me formulate and solidify content through countless discussions regarding personal finances.

My children are reserved a special place in heaven for putting up with a father who, among other faults, obsesses about financial concepts and can't help but to see the world through fiscal lenses.

My wife, Jennifer, deserves special praise and mention for putting up with two years of on-again, off-again writing and musings. She was kind enough to act as the sounding board for much of the book's content, design, and direction.

Finally, my gratitude goes out to my young daughter, who allowed me to use her "Smiley Guy" character for the book's illustrations. She spent considerable time sketching concepts and converting them into digital form. Without those illustrations, the book would lose so much of its light-hearted appeal.

www.ingramcontent.com/pod-product-compliance
Lightning Source LLC
Chambersburg PA
CBHW032016190326
41520CB00007B/493

www.ingramcontent.com/pod-product-compliance
Lightning Source LLC
Chambersburg PA
CBHW032016190326
41520CB00007B/493